A Golden Adventure

The Hunt for the Missing Rainbow

To: Jessica

Happy Reading!
Sarah Beebe

Sarah Beebe

First printing, 2016

Printed in the United States of America

For permission requests, contact the author at www.skbpublishing.com.

ISBN: 154053376X
ISBN-13: 978-1540533760

For my beautiful daughters, Lila and Alexis, who love spending time in nature and

looking for rainbows!

For my amazingly supportive husband, Eric. Thank you for always believing in me!

Finally, for my two sweet goldens, Sunni and Goldie, who love life and teach me every day to enjoy

the simple pleasures that life has to offer!

A Golden Adventure

The Hunt for the Missing Rainbow

Two goldens walking on a bright sunny day.

Goldie runs excitedly to see a rainbow along the way.

The older golden, Sunni, races

to catch up,

but sees the rainbow has faded

and left one sad pup.

Sunni who is older and can be a

little blunt,

tells Goldie to cheer up, they

will go on a rainbow hunt.

So off the goldens go,

running to and fro.

As they hike together, juicy
apples appear.

"Red! The first color in the
rainbow," Goldie cheers.

Sunni spots some beautiful

butterflies.

"Orange! The second color in

the rainbow," Goldie cries.

Goldie feeling excited about all the colors they've found, shouts, "Yellow! The third color in the rainbow," as she runs around.

After all this running, they spot

a field to take a nap.

"Green! The fourth color in the

rainbow," Goldie yaps.

After they awake, the pups raise their cheeks.

"Blue! The fifth color in the rainbow," Goldie squeaks.

Running through the meadow,

their excitement grows.

Goldie squeals, "Violet! The

sixth color in the rainbow!"

The rain begins to sprinkle and

the sun peeks out.

They run and bark excitedly as

Goldie shouts…

"We found the missing rainbow!"

Making Reading Fun Connection

After sharing this story with your favorite readers, take them on their own rainbow hunt. See if they can find all the colors in the rainbow. Take pictures of what they find or bring a clipboard and coloring supplies to draw the objects while you explore the colors of the rainbow together. Enjoy!